My Little

Washington, DC

By Rich Volin
Illustrated by Ed Myer

A GOLDEN BOOK • NEW YORK

Text copyright © 2021 by Penguin Random House LLC
Cover and interior illustrations copyright © 2021 by Ed Myer
All rights reserved. Published in the United States by Golden Books, an imprint of Random House Children's Books, a division of Penguin Random House LLC, 1745 Broadway, New York, NY 10019. Golden Books, A Golden Book, A Little Golden Book, the G colophon, and the distinctive gold spine are registered trademarks of Penguin Random House LLC.
rhcbooks.com
Educators and librarians, for a variety of teaching tools, visit us at RHTeachersLibrarians.com
Library of Congress Control Number: 2020934948
ISBN 978-0-593-30115-9 (trade) — ISBN 978-0-593-30116-6 (ebook)
Printed in the United States of America
10 9 8 7 6 5 4 3 2 1

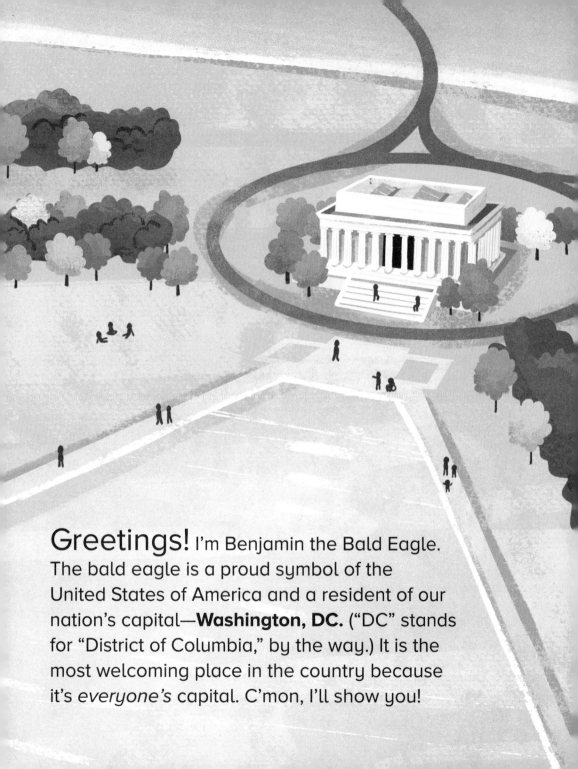

Greetings! I'm Benjamin the Bald Eagle. The bald eagle is a proud symbol of the United States of America and a resident of our nation's capital—**Washington, DC.** ("DC" stands for "District of Columbia," by the way.) It is the most welcoming place in the country because it's *everyone's* capital. C'mon, I'll show you!

Let's start with some of the most impressive museums in the world. I'm a big fan of the **National Museum of Natural History**.

Here you'll learn about animals, plants, and other natural wonders that have existed throughout Earth's history. You can gaze at massive mammals, explore human evolution, and even stroll among *real* butterflies in the Butterfly Pavilion.

Nearby is the **National Museum of American History,** which has collected nearly two million historical objects and cultural treasures from our country's past.

You can see the Star-Spangled Banner—the tattered American flag that flew over Fort McHenry in 1814 and inspired our national anthem.

Or check out the ruby slippers worn by Dorothy in the classic movie *The Wizard of Oz.*

I always like to fly by the **National Air and Space Museum** to take in all kinds of aviation marvels, from the pioneering planes that first left the ground to the spectacular spacecraft that left the atmosphere.

I can soar high, but this is really impressive!

All are welcome at the **National Museum of African American History and Culture**. Learn about African American music and sports icons, artists and educators, and the heroes who fought to give every American the rights they deserve!

DC is also home to some of the greatest monuments in the world—each built with the hope that YOU will drop by! Some, like the **Martin Luther King, Jr. Memorial**, celebrate the leaders who inspired our nation.

The impressive **Lincoln Memorial** is dedicated to our sixteenth president, Abraham Lincoln.

From the top of the steps, visitors can enjoy an amazing view of the reflecting pool that stretches from the base of the stairs. You can also see the huge **Lincoln Statue**, which is 19 feet tall and weighs 175 tons!

From museums to monuments, that's a lot of learning. And there's no need to stop yet! Head to the **Bureau of Engraving and Printing** to see how paper money is made. *Billions* of dollars are printed there every year.

Hey, that handsome fella looks just like me!

That was exciting! I need a moment to relax on the **Metro**, a sprawling rail system that can take you anywhere you want to go in DC and beyond. Maybe I'll ride the train someplace where I can take a walk and reconnect with, say . . .

. . . PANDAS! No tour of DC is complete without a romp through the **National Zoo** and a visit with my favorite black-and-white furry friends!

The National Zoo was founded way back in 1889 and is spread across more than 160 acres. It's home to around 2,700 animals from nearly 400 different species.

Let's stay outdoors and head over to the **Tidal Basin**, where thousands of people come each spring to see one of the largest displays of **cherry blossoms** in the world.

Many visitors also take in the view of the domed **Jefferson Memorial** from a paddleboat. (Personally, I prefer to fly.)

Next, let's take a stroll around the corner to the **National Mall**. Don't worry—I'm not talking about a bunch of stores inside a *shopping* mall. Our Mall is a huge park with a long grassy field that goes right through the middle of DC. And it's easy to find—just look for the **Washington Monument**!

The Mall is a great place to relax and play, or to hold a special event, like the annual Blossom Kite Festival.

That was fun, but it's time to get back to business. And this town knows business! Washington, DC, is the center of our nation's government. Your elected representatives from around the country all meet in the **United States Capitol** to debate and vote on our laws. No wonder the building has more than five hundred rooms!

Understanding and interpreting our laws is the job of the **Supreme Court of the United States**—the highest court in the land. While court is in session, you can even watch as the nine justices hear a case!

EQUAL JUSTICE UNDER LAW

Meanwhile, the president of the United States is also working—across town in the **White House**! Every US president except one has lived in this majestic mansion. Can you guess which one? (I'll give you a hint: He has the same name as the city we've been exploring!)

When the workday is done, there's nothing more enjoyable for this local bird than to root, root, root for the home team at **Nationals Park**! Let's go, Nats!

What a day! I hope you've enjoyed the bird's-eye view. And remember: Washington, DC, is *your* nation's capital—which makes it *everyone's* hometown! Maybe one day you'll bring your own kids to see this historic place.